MW01625731

Cici.B
THE CRIMSON KISS

GET YOUR

Sh*t Together

JOURNAL PROMPTS & QUOTES FOR SOME SERIOUS REFLECTION & GROWTH

Cici B

Self-work isn't easy, and it's not meant to fix your whole life overnight. Unpacking deep emotions, confronting yourself, coming face to to face with certain realizations about yourself that you never knew existed - all of these things can be really overwhelming, difficult, exhausting, and shocking - so remember to give yourself grace and take things at your pace. Whether you crawl some days or are able to run others, always be proud of yourself for moving forward.

Don't hold back with these prompts, sis.

Spill your fucking guts out.

B

When you realize that something no longer serves you, or aligns with the life you're in the process of building for yourself, thank it for the lessons it taught you, then send it on its way... out of your life.

Things on my mind

Date:

Deep breath

Today I'm letting go of thoughts and beliefs that do not serve the version of myself that I'm working towards stepping into; those thoughts and beliefs are:

So many of us grew up in broken homes and environments, and didn't have any examples of self-love, weren't taught to put ourselves first, weren't taught to practice self-care - you aren't alone.

Forgive yourself for all the things you've been struggling with or getting wrong because no one taught you how to do them right, or at all.

Things on my mind

Date:

Not my fault

Today I'm forgiving myself for the things that I have been struggling with, and/or have gotten wrong because no one ever taught me how to do them right, or do them at all; those things are:

Putting myself first

Knowing my worth.

You owe it to yourself
to be good to yourself.

No *excuses.*

Things on my mind

Date:

I Deserve

Today I'm reminding myself of all the things I am deserving of; those things are:

Being a giver is a beautiful thing, but you have to make sure the people you choose to be a part of your life are also givers, because no matter how big your heart is, sis... you deserve and need to be replenished, too.

Things on my mind

Date:

Baby girl...

If I could go back in time and have a conversation with my younger self, these are all the things I would tell her:

Dump him

move - anywhere

Do what brings Joy

don't chase $

Treat yourself the way you
want others to treat you.
Love on yourself the way you
want others to love on you.
You set the bar, sis.
You set the tone.
You set the energy.
YOU.

Things on my mind

Date:

I know better

Today I'm listing all of the areas in my life that I know I can and should be doing better in, but am not, writing out the reasons why, then being honest with myself as to whether or not those reasons are valid, or if they are actually excuses:

It is not the responsibility of others to "make" you happy, or be your peace; it is your responsibility to unlock those things within yourself.

Things on my mind

Date:

Me vs Me

Today I'm writing honestly about the woman I am right now, vs the woman I want to be for myself, then listing all of the things I know that I need to do in order to become the woman I want to be for myself:

You can inspire others to change for the better by being better for yourself, but you cannot make anyone change.

Things on my mind

Date:

Today I'm writing a letter to the person who hurt me (past or present), and I'm going to say all of the things that I've always wanted to, but never did.
This letter will be unapologetic, and I will not hold back.
"Dear ____, I want you to know":

Forget about everything else- building a healthy relationship with yourself needs to be your number one priority 'cause girlfriend, lemme tell ya...

when you're not good on the inside, that shit will always show up on the outside.

Things on my mind

Date:

Mic check, 1-2.

Today I'm checking in with myself - How am I feeling and why? What do I really want in my life and why? What do I need in my life and why? Have I been taking care of myself? (If you have been taking care of yourself, list all the ways, if you haven't been, write the reasons why):

You will continue to confuse confidence with arrogance if you don't step into your own self-love. You're supposed to big yourself up. You're supposed to fuck with yourself the real way. You're supposed to be proud of yourself.

Things on my mind

Date:

I'm pretty lit

Today I'm giving myself compliments and I'm patting myself on the back for doing and/or being all of these things:

Taking responsibility for ourselves and our lives is also self-love.

Things on my mind

Date:

Grown woman shit

Today I am listing 3 ways that I can start being more responsible for myself, along with how they will benefit me now, and in the longrun:

Being the "bigger person" does not mean allowing others to walk all over you just to "keep the peace".

Being the bigger person means standing up for yourself and holding others accountable for their shitty behaviour by telling them about it, then removing yourself from them if need be.

Things on my mind

Date:

Boundaries, baby

Today I'm checking in on my boundaries by making a list of each one, then putting a "✓" beside the ones that I have been respecting, and an " ✕ " besides the ones I haven't. Then, for all of the boundaries that I haven't been respecting, I'm writing the reasons why, along with some things I know I need to do in order to strengthen them.

My sis,
when you know in your heart that something is not your fault, don't apologize for it, and don't allow anyone to try to make you feel like you should.

Things on my mind

Date:

Today I'm confronting any and all things I do that relate to people pleasing by listing them all, then beside or under each one, writing why I feel the need to do them.
Then, I'm reflecting on where those needs originated from, writing them down, and also writing the things I can start practicing to break the habit of people pleasing.

Not having the space to take on
the loads of other people
is not, "letting them down"-
it's you, respecting your own
loads that you're trying to work
through.

It's you, respecting your mental,
emotional, and spiritual health.

Things on my mind

Date:

Protecting myself

In order to protect my peace and continue to elevate, there are certain people with specific character traits that I need to stay away from; those specific character traits are:

Drop the phrase, "Easier said than done" which does nothing to help raise your vibrations, and replace it with, "It'll be hard, but gawt damn it, I'm gonna do it!" - because that's what is going to raise your vibrations and inspire you to get shit done.

Things on my mind

Date:

Today I'm making a bucket list and I'm including everything. From the smallest thing I want to do, to the biggest, most wildest thing - I'm not leaving anything out:

You always have the power to bounce back stronger and better than ever, sis... always.

Date:

Today I'm writing whatever is in my heart/on my mind:

*Girlfriend,
another woman's "no" is a complete sentence for you, too. Just like men, you are also not entitled to anything she isn't already offering you - this includes, but is not limited to - advice, therapy sessions, emotional and/or physical labour, and an explanation as to why she is saying no.
Give another woman the same respect you would like her to give you.*

Things on my mind

Date:

Checking myself

Today I'm checking in on the way I behave when it comes to another woman's boundaries (both strangers off and online, and women I know personally). When another woman tells me "no", do I respect it, or do I *disrespect* her by trying to guilt trip, or manipulate her into changing her mind?
Do I feel entitled to another woman's time, energy, resources, and emotional labour? If yes, why?
Do I unload my problems on to other women without first asking if they have they space?

*I remember how I used to
constantly dim my own light
when I saw that others felt
like theirs wasn't bright
enough while around me...
yeah, not anymore and never
again.
I refuse to keep "friends" in
my life who are too insecure
to grasp the concept of shining
brightly together.*

Things on my mind

Date:

This big light of mine

Today I'm taking a closer look at the people I call friends. Are they truly friends to me, or am I only a friend to them? Are there friends in my life that I feel like I always have to walk on eggshells around? Are there friends in my life that I feel like I can't celebrate my accomplishments with, or around? Are there friends in my life that I feel are jealous of me? Are there friends in my life who I've noticed always have to find a way to take the "spotlight" off of me, or others, to focus it on themselves? Are there friends in my life who project their insecurities on to me often? (If yes to any or all of these questions, write about the things they do/ways they behave that make you feel that way, then ask yourself why you keep these people in your life.)

For some people it takes courage to go after their dreams, for others, it takes courage just to get out of bed in the morning and face the world - both are achievements worthy of celebrating - so no matter what the move you make in your life is, celebrate that shit, girl.

Things on my mind

Date:

Credit to myself is Due

Today I'm celebrating my progress by listing all the obstacles
- big or small - that I've overcome this year;
those obstacles were:

You can learn so much
from the cautionary tales
of other women;
you don't always need
to walk the same paths as
them in order to pick up
the same lessons.

Things on my mind

Date:

Today I'm writing a letter to a woman who inspires me to be the best version of myself. Dear____:

Let the lowest point you've ever been inspire you to rise higher than you've ever risen.

Things on my mind

Date:

Plot twist

Today I'm reframing. I'm finding positives in situations I have only been looking at negatively.

Example: "This hurt me, but it also taught me_____, and because of that lesson, I now know _____."

"This shitty thing is happening at the moment, but I know that_____."

It's been said that in life, whatever we feed grows and whatever we let starve dies. Ask yourself:

Which parts of yourself have you been feeding - and with what - and which parts of yourself have you been letting starve?

Things on my mind

Date:

Nutrition check

Honestly, no bullshit: Which parts of myself have I been feeding - and with what - and which parts of myself have I been letting starve?

(Note: This prompt is about taking a look at your mental, emotional, and spiritual health - not actual food - but if you want/need to include that, by all means, do so.)

Someone else's success
will never take away
from your own, love.
There truly is room
for all of us.

Things on my mind

Date:

Moving off of Jealousy Ave

Today I'm writing about the person (or people) that I am jealous of, then listing the reasons why. From there, I'm self-reflecting by writing about the things I feel like I'm lacking in my own life that drives me to be jealous, and the changes I need to make or things I need to accomplish in my own life so that I don't need to feel that way anymore:

Doing inner work is probably one of the highest forms of self-love, in my opinion. The more work you do, the more aligned with yourself you'll get, and the more aligned with yourself you get, the easier it will be to remove yourself from people who aren't for you, and cut ties with the version of yourself that no longer serves you.

Things on my mind

Date:

Spilling hot tea

Today I'm zeroing in on the areas of my life that I know need more work; those areas are:

Health
- Diet
- Exercise

Body
- Yoga
- Hike.
- Rollerskate

- Mental
  - Art
  - Clean house (actually clean the house)
- Invest $ on beautiful surroundings

There is always a solution,
beloved...

you just have to be willing
to find, or make one for
yourself.

Things on my mind

Date:

Claiming it from now!

Today I'm writing out some goals. Whether those goals are short or long term, I'm writing them out and claiming them as already being mine.

Example: "Next year I'm buying that condo - no excuses. That condo is mine. Claiming it from now!"

*Trying to rush through
every chapter of your life
just to get to the next one is
only a disservice to yourself;
it's okay to slow down and
take your time so that you
can really pay attention to
what's going on in each.
Your life is not a race my
love...*

it is a true journey.

Things on my mind

Date:

Oh. Hey there, self-care

Today I'm writing all of the things I need and want to do for myself, but have been neglecting by using the excuse, "I don't have time". After I've written them out, I'm going to **make** time for each, because taking care of myself is fucking important. (Note: These can be things like, "Reading more." "Spending more time with myself." "Taking or finishing an online class.")

You can ask people what they think you should do until you're blue in the face, but at the end of the day, you are the one that has to live with the consequences of the decisions you make - not them.
From now on, rather than constantly asking everyone how to live your life, start putting more trust in yourself, and do what feels right for you.

Things on my mind

Date:

My truth about trust

Today I'm writing about trust. What does trust mean to me? Do I trust the people in my life right now? If not, why? And why do I allow them to be in my life if I don't trust them? Do I trust myself? If not, why? Who taught me not to trust myself? Where do my trust issues stem from?

Own your truths

x

Set yourself free.

Things on my mind

Date:

Unpacking my shit

Today I'm unpacking my feelings of resentment and bitterness. Who have I been holding resentment for in my heart, and why? How long have I been holding on to this? What was the defining situation that launched me into a bitter place, and why has it taken me so long to address it with myself? Now that all of my truths are on the table for me to see clearly, if they were someone else's truths, what advice would I give to them in terms of moving forward and healing?

Hi, it's me, B :)

So, I know that a lot of these prompts were probably really hard because they forced you to confront feelings and thoughts that you've been avoiding, or didn't know you needed to confront at all - and if no one told you today, let me tell you...
I'm fucking proud of you.

This self-work shit is NOT easy, but trust me when I say, it's so worth it, and we all deserve it from ourselves.

I'm going to leave you with some "lighter" prompts for the next few pages so that you can just vibe out. Please remember to big up yourself, and always know... you got this.

Much love, Boo.

xo

3 quotes that changed my life for the better:

The best advice I've ever gotten from another woman is:

The best advice I've ever gotten from a man is:

3 qualities about myself that I'm grateful for:

3 people in my life that I'm grateful for:

I love when people compliment me on these 3 things:

3 things I want to master the art of:

Something I wish more people in the world would do more of:

Something I wish more people in the world would do less of:

A piece of advice I always give to others, but often forget to use for myself:

3 things I believe every woman should always remember:

3 things I believe every man should always remember:

Things on my mind

Letters to My Ex

Blush

Spilled Words: The Crimson Kiss Quote Collection

Lost and Found: The Book of Short Stories

Girl Power: The Crimson Kiss Quote Collection II

12:02AM: Exploring B (short erotica)

The Self-Love Bible: How I Learned to Love Myself

Big Sis Talks: The Crimson Kiss Quote Collection III

How I Built My Author Brand on Instagram

Sis, Get your Sh*t Together
(Struggle-Love Edition)

www.AuthorCiciB.com
Instagram: TheCrimsonKiss

Cinque Terre 3
~~Pisa~~

Florence 3
*Pisa (Day trip)

(Day trip.) San gimig ano

sienna
*naples.

Rome 3
(Pensione (Room)) vatican

Amalfi Coast 5
Amalfi Hotel

Made in the USA
Middletown, DE
21 January 2021